Anchored in Self-Control

A Fruit of the Spirit Devotional for kids

JENNA MAYE THOMPSON

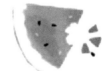

Anchored in Self Control

A Fruit of the Spirit devotional for kids.

JENNA MAYE THOMPSON

INDEX

1
What is Self-Control

"**22** But the fruit of the Spirit is love, joy, peace, forbearance, kindness, goodness, faithfulness, **23** gentleness and self-control. Against such things there is no law."
Galatians 5:22-23

Have you ever heard of the fruits of the Spirit before? It is a term in the Bible that references *nine* **(9)** different qualities that a person who knows and loves God can receive from the Holy Spirit.

Are you picturing apples and bananas right now?
Me, too!

But what this verse is actually referring to is **fruit** being the result of hard work. Today we use the term "the fruit of our labor" to communicate the results of our effort.

Do you understand what the word "fruit" in this verse means now?

It's so meaningful!

When we let the Holy Spirit work in our lives, the result is having love, joy, peace, patience, kindness, goodness, faithfulness, gentleness, and **self-control!**

We will be studying **self-control** and how to apply it to our lives to see a bountiful "harvest"!

Are you ready?

A Fruit of the Spirit

~Time to Pray~

Lord, thank you for the gift of the Holy Spirit. I pray that You would open up my heart and mind so that I can receive the fantastic gifts You have to offer. Help me learn to have self-control and show me how to apply it in my life. Thank you for Your help.

Amen.

SELF-CONTROL SCENARIOS

Can you think of a scenario in which you would need to use self-control?

What should you do if a grown-up tells you to clean your bedroom and you really don't want to?

If your sister or brother reached over and colored all over your schoolwork and you really wanted to yell at him/her, how could you use self-control at that moment?

2
You Can Do It!

"7 For the Spirit God gave us does not make us timid, but gives us power, love and self-discipline."
2 Timothy 1:7

Sometimes, using **self-control** can put us in challenging situations. Because **we are followers of Jesus**, we hold ourselves to certain standards, always trying to do what God wants us to do.

He allows us to have friends who aren't Christians in our lives. But you need to always remember that, sometimes, those friends don't know how to act like Jesus because they don't really know him. They may ask us to do things that we know Jesus wouldn't want us to do, such as watching a movie we shouldn't watch, listening to a song with

A Fruit of the Spirit

inappropriate lyrics, making fun of or bullying another kid, or maybe even lying to our parents!

*It is our job to stand strong in what we believe and tell our friends **we can't** participate in certain activities!*

This is **hard**, but **not impossible!**

We need to use the gift of self-control, and God is here to help. The Bible verse in this lesson tells us that the Holy Spirit in us is not timid. He is powerful and strong and helps us to have self-control and to do what is right.

The Holy Spirit speaks to us through the words in the Bible and nudges our hearts, helping us make the right decisions.

Make sure you're always listening!

~Time to Pray~

Lord, I want to thank You for always being with me and helping me in hard situations. When I need help in standing strong and having self-control, I ask that You will speak to me and show me what to do or say. Help me be a good example to my friends and family so that I can show them who You are through my actions!

Amen.

SELF-CONTROL SCENARIOS

What should you do if you're at a friend's house and they turn on a tv show or movie that you know you're not allowed to watch?

If a friend at school says a word that you know you shouldn't say and there are no adults around to hear it, should you say it as well?

(Remember: God is always listening)

A Fruit of the Spirit

3
Overcoming Temptation

"**18** For I know that good itself does not dwell in me, that is, in my sinful nature. For I have the desire to do what is good, but I cannot carry it out."

Romans 7:18

There is nothing more frustrating than knowing exactly what you're supposed to be doing yet feeling like you just can't do it!

For example, Sophie knew that it wasn't right to be mean to her little sister, but she always seemed to be forgetting and doing it anyway. One day, she was feeling kind of grumpy and really wanted to be alone, but her sister wanted to play.

She kept begging Sophie to come out of her room and play, and Sophie lost control. She yelled at her sister to go away, and that made her sister so sad!

Sophie needed help. She had a lack of *self-control* and knew she needed to be more patient.

What should you do *when you know you're not supposed to do something, but you're having trouble saying 'no'?*

Pray!

Ask Jesus!

He is our helper.

We were born sinners, but we also have God in us, helping us to resist temptation. Sometimes, it isn't easy to do the right thing. Sometimes we don't have the strength to do it on our own. But you must remember that we get to call out to Jesus for help when we are going through that difficult time.

He is always there to help us and can transform us and make us perfect in His sight.

Thank you, Jesus!

A Fruit of the Spirit

~Time to Pray~

Jesus, You know my heart and the things that I struggle with. Sometimes, I have a hard time choosing to do the right thing. Please speak to me and guide me in the right direction. When I am tempted to do the wrong thing, speak to me, and show me how to say no! Thank you for transforming my life into a life that is pleasing to You.

Amen!

SELF-CONTROL SCENARIOS

Have you ever lost control and yelled at your sister or brother? What should you do the next time you feel frustrated like that?

Let's pretend that your mom has told you to stop fighting with your sister or brother several times, and your sister just said something that made you really mad. How could you use self-control in this situation?

4
Everything in Moderation

"²⁷ It is not good to eat too much honey,
nor is it honorable to search out matters that are
too deep.
²⁸ Like a city whose walls are broken through
is a person who lacks self-control."
Proverbs 25:27-28

Do you like honey?

What about cookies?

How about donuts?

There is nothing wrong with these tasty treats. But, too much of something usually isn't good for you. If you eat too many donuts, you will probably have a stomachache and won't feel very good.

Sometimes, it's tough to stop eating something delicious, isn't it? You think to yourself, "I've already had two (2); I'll just have one (1) more!" *But that is how the devil works.* He urges us to go a little farther than we should, and then a little farther until we just go too far!

That's not very nice, is it?

We need to practice standing firm and learn when to say enough is enough.

Thank goodness we have a good God who is always there to help, right? When you're tempted to go a little too far, just stop and say a quick little prayer.

Ask the Holy Spirit to give you strength and self-control!

Remember, you are strong because you have Jesus. He will be your strength when you are weak.

Just ask!

~Time to Pray~

Lord, please help me to have **self-control** in my daily life. Please help me make good decisions even when I really don't want to. I know that you will reward me for choosing what is right. Give me discernment when I'm making decisions and help me to continue to learn right from wrong. I love you, Lord!

Amen.

SELF-CONTROL SCENARIOS

Is there a game you really like to play on a phone or tablet? Have you ever spent too much time playing it? Games are a lot of fun, but sometimes they keep us from doing more important things like our homework, cleaning our room, or reading our Bible.

What do you think would be a **reasonable** time limit to set for yourself from now on?

upright and Holy

"**11** For the grace of God has appeared that offers salvation to all people. **12** It teaches us to say "No" to ungodliness and worldly passions, and to live self-controlled, upright and godly lives in this present age,"
Titus 2:11-12

We are so blessed with God's gift of grace! He has forgiven our sins before we've even committed them. He chose to die on the cross even while knowing the sins we were going to commit in the future.

Wow!

But that doesn't mean that we can just go around doing whatever we want, does it?

No, it doesn't.

He wants us to live according to His commands, and when we mess up, we have to come to Him in repentance and confess our sins.

He will always forgive us.

As we learn and grow, we will become more aware of what is ungodly and say 'no' to those things. We will learn how to have self-control and be upright and holy even in this crazy world we live in.

If you want to live a life full of God's blessings, start asking God to change your heart.

If your heart is right, your actions will follow.

So let's work on getting our hearts aligned with God so that our actions and words will reflect Him!

~Time to Pray~

Lord, I pray that You would show me the things that I need to change in my life so that I can be more pleasing to You. I pray that you would cleanse my heart and make it pure. *Thank you* for dying on the cross for my sins; I know that I don't deserve that, and I am so grateful. Help me show my gratitude by having self-control and saying 'no' to wrong and ungodly things.

Amen.

SELF-CONTROL SCENARIOS

An excellent example of being upright and holy is refraining from gossiping—talking badly about someone when they aren't around.

What should you do if your friend leans over and tells you that she thinks your other friend is mean?

If someone came up and told you a big secret about someone else and told you not to tell and then, later on, you really wanted to tell another friend, would it be considered gossiping to tell then?

Anchored in Self Control

6

Always Moving Forward

"⁵ For this very reason, make every effort to add to your faith goodness; and to goodness, knowledge; ⁶ and to knowledge, self-control; and to self-control, perseverance; and to perseverance, godliness; ⁷ and to godliness, mutual affection; and to mutual affection, love."

2 Peter 1:5-7

Becoming a Christian isn't the end of the road. We've still got work to do. Jesus wants us to always be working toward Godliness.

We are so blessed to have The Bible *teach us all of what He wants us to know and do.*

A Fruit of the Spirit

The verse above is very clear in telling us what the Lord expects from us.

Did you notice that one of the qualities that Jesus would like us to add to our faith is Self-Control?

We have been learning that it is so essential to have Self-Control to be productive in our faith and to be able to show people how Jesus is transforming our lives.

We need to be actively working toward being more and more like Jesus. Continue to ask the Lord for help. He will take it very seriously and show you ways that you can grow in Him!

You are strong because Jesus is in you!

Don't ever forget that.

~Time to Pray~

God, thank you for giving us the Bible so that I can learn and grow to be more like You. Please help me to be more Godly, to have more self-control, and love as You do. Please continue to show me ways to improve and help me be strong when I feel weak and tempted to give in to temptation. *Thank you*, because I know that I can come to You when I need help.

Amen.

SELF-CONTROL SCENARIOS

It's so important to always be learning more about God and becoming more like Him. Sometimes, it takes self-control to put down your toys or games and pick up your Bible. What are some things you could do that would help you remember to read your Bible and pray more?

Jesus understands

"**10** Jesus said to him, "Away from me, Satan! For it is written: 'Worship the Lord your God, and serve him only.'" "

Matthew 4:10

Temptation is the keen desire to do something, especially something wrong or unwise.

Do you think Jesus has ever been tempted?

He has!

The Bible says that Satan tempted Jesus for 40 days! Satan wanted Jesus to worship *him*! During this time, Jesus chose to fast from eating so that he could focus on what was ahead.

Do you know what Satan did? He tempted Jesus with food and tried to get Him to lose His **self-control!** *Do you think Jesus gave in?*

No way!

Instead, He used Bible verses to explain to Satan why He wasn't going to bow down to him. He quoted Matthew 4:10 and told him that He would only worship God. Satan gave up and left.

Jesus was victorious!

If the devil can try to tempt even Jesus (don't worry, he will never be successful), then he can undoubtedly tempt us!

One way he uses to tempt us is through studying our habits. For example: If we find something that we think is pretty or cool but doesn't belong to us, the devil will do what he can to put us in situations that will make us want to take it for ourselves. That is what we call being tempted to steal. **And stealing is not good.**

A Fruit of the Spirit

Sometimes, it's really hard to have Self-Control, isn't it?

Did you know that you have the Holy Spirit who can help you? All you have to do is pray and ask for His help. You can be victorious!

You will be victorious because you have all of the help anyone could ever ask for. Jesus.

~Time to Pray~

Lord, thank you for being such a great example of self-control. Please help me to be strong and victorious and to do things according to Your will! When Satan is tempting me, I pray that You will help me be aware of it and immediately ask the Holy Spirit for help and guidance. Thank you for teaching me how to be more like You. In Jesus' name, Amen!

SELF-CONTROL SCENARIOS

What would you do if you were at a store and a small toy you were wanting had fallen off of the shelf?

What if your parent was distracted and you knew if you were to put it in your pocket, no one would see?

Would you steal it? Be honest! If the answer is yes, talk to your trusted adult and pray and ask Jesus to help you have **self-control** when you're tempted.

Always a Way Out

"[13] No temptation has overtaken you except what is common to mankind. And God is faithful; he will not let you be tempted beyond what you can bear. But when you are tempted, he will also provide a way out so that you can endure it."
1 Corinthians 10:13

Have you ever been in a really hard situation and felt like no one could understand how you're feeling? A little boy named Jonah was.

Do you want to hear about how he practiced self-control?

Jonah had a sweet tooth, which means that he really loved sugary treats. He was allowed to have a little treat after dinner every night, and one particular day his mom had made brownies! Those were his absolute favorite. He couldn't wait to have one.

As Jonah walked to the plate of brownies, the devil began to tempt him. Jonah knew that he was alone in the room, and nobody would know if he took more than one.

He reached for a brownie and quickly ate it—it was delicious! Then, he slowly reached for another. But, all of a sudden, he felt something in his spirit urging him to put it back.

It was the Holy Spirit helping him!

Jonah listened to the Holy Spirit's prompting, and he put the brownie back. At that moment, he practiced self-control.

Obeying your parents and doing what is right always feels better than one little moment of worldly satisfaction.

Don't you agree?

~Time to Pray~

Lord, I praise you and thank you for all that you do for me. I thank you for the gift of the Holy Spirit who helps me in times of temptation. Please help me to always be aware of His prompting and to be strong enough to listen. Nothing is impossible through You, Jesus.

Amen.

SELF-CONTROL SCENARIOS

Do you like brownies and cookies?

What if someone made some and left them on the counter with the instructions not to touch them and left the room? That would be really tempting. You already know that you shouldn't sneak the treats. So, what are some things you can do to distract yourself and do the right thing?

9
Set Aside Your Idols

"³² Better a patient person than a warrior,
one with self-control than one who takes a city."
Proverbs 16:32

The world tries to tell us that being popular and wealthy are the most essential qualities to have. They make us feel like we need more money, all of the best toys, the most friends, and the best clothes.

Have you ever felt that way?

We all have!

Did you know that this world is not our forever home? This is all just temporary. But, wait a

A Fruit of the Spirit

second, you must be wondering that if this world is not our home, where is our forever home?

Heaven!

We are created in God's image, and we are called to spend eternity with Him in Heaven!

Jesus is our King. Jesus is the one that we are supposed to "impress," and He doesn't care if we have the best toys or cutest clothes.

He cares about our hearts and our actions.

He wants our lives to be pleasing to *him*.

There is nothing wrong with wearing nice clothes and having a lot of friends! Those things are just a fun part of living this life. However, God does not want us to idolize these things.

Do you know what that means?

It's when you love or admire something a little too much.

God should be our number one priority, so the next time you find yourself putting your friendships, favorite hobbies, or your favorite game before God, remember that He gave you self-control.

use it!

*Set aside the things that are distracting you from God and turn your eyes to **Him.***

~Time to Pray~

Lord, please show me the things that have become so important to me and have distracted me from spending time with You and learning to be more like You. Give me self-control so that I can limit my time thinking about these things. Please help me fix my eyes on you and turn my thoughts to heavenly things.

Amen.

A Fruit of the Spirit

SELF-CONTROL SCENARIOS

A little girl named Maggie really wanted a new coat that all of her friends had. However, her mom said she couldn't have it because she already had a perfectly good coat. Maggie yelled and screamed and acted very mean to her mom.

It made her mom really sad!

Is that how she should have responded?

How would you have responded?

10

Keep Your Tongue From Evil

"The tongue has the power of life and death, and those who love it will eat its fruit."
Proverbs 18:21

Has someone ever made you so angry that you just wanted to yell and scream at them? We are born sinners, so that has probably happened to all of us before. It's not our best side, is it? It makes everyone involved feel bad, and it just isn't productive! Often, the words will just fly out of our mouths before we have time to stop them.

Did you know that we can actually control that impulsive urge? ***It's not easy, but we can train***

A Fruit of the Spirit

ourselves to have **self-control** *and keep our tongues from evil.*

When we are trying to do something hard, it is helpful to understand why it's important first.

Do you know why controlling what you say is so important?

The Bible says that the tongue and what comes out of your mouth actually has the power of life and death.

Wow.

You were put on this earth for a reason.

You are called and chosen to show people who God is and help them draw near to Him.

Do you think that if you are always being grouchy and speaking angrily to those around you, they will see Jesus in You and want to be close to Him? No. That is not likely.

However, if you practice **self-control** and choose patience and kind words in moments of frustration, you will imitate God and His image and will also be doing what You were made to do. To glorify Him. That is an extraordinary calling, and Jesus will help you every step of the way.

Anchored in Self Control

~Time to Pray~

Thank you, Jesus, that You have called and anointed me to be a follower of You. I am so thankful that you chose me. I pray that You will give me the gift of **self-control** so that I may use my words to bring people to You and further Your kingdom. Use me, Lord.

Amen.

SELF-CONTROL SCENARIOS

What would you do if you were riding in the car next to your brother or sister, and they kept on poking you over and over again even after you asked them to stop? That would really make you want to lose your temper, wouldn't it?

What is one thing you could do to calm down and have self-control?

A Fruit of the Spirit

11

Slow to Anger

"¹⁹ My dear brothers and sisters, take note of this: Everyone should be quick to listen, slow to speak and slow to become angry,"
James 1:19

Have you ever had someone be unkind to you?

Have you had someone say something mean to you?

That's really hard.

How do you think we should respond when someone treats us unfairly? Should we say something mean to them? Should we "get them back" and do to them what they did to us?

Jesus wants to help us in hard situations like this. He says that we should be slow to anger and wants us to use **self-control** to "zip up our lips." Do you know what that means?

It means that words don't fly out!

Can you practice zipping up your lips?

If someone says something unkind to you, you can use your God-given **self-control** to walk away without responding in anger. Today, as you're going about your day, do your best to be slow to anger, be patient, and practice **self-control**.

Zip up those lips!

~Time to Pray~

Lord, I pray that You would help me use **self-control** in times where I feel frustrated and want to say something unkind. I thank You for Your gift of grace and for forgiving me when I mess up. Be with me today as I work on being patient and controlling what I say.

Amen.

A Fruit of the Spirit

SELF-CONTROL SCENARIOS

Let's say you're trying to focus on your homework, but your little sister keeps singing loudly, making it **really hard** to focus! Your first instinct is to yell at her and tell her to be quiet.

Would that actually help? Or would it just make her sad or angry?

What could you nicely say to get her to quiet down and let you work?

12
Overlooking Insults

"16 Fools show their annoyance at once,
but the prudent overlook an insult."
Proverbs 12:16

What do you think the word 'prudent' means? **It means to show care and thought for the future.**

In Proverbs, this verse says that it is foolish to show your annoyance when someone does something that offends you.

The verse also says that a prudent person overlooks an insult. Always remember that Jesus wants us to remain calm when someone says something that we don't like.

A Fruit of the Spirit

Have you ever gotten angry and said something unkind and then regretted it later because it hurt somebody's feelings?

Or maybe you didn't even really mean those words, but it was too late to take them back.

That is why Jesus says to be prudent and think about the future and how your words and actions will affect others. Most likely, after you've calmed down, you'll be able to overlook the insult, and you won't have hurt anyone in the process.

It isn't easy being patient and remaining calm when someone hurts your feelings.

You are probably going to mess up sometimes because no one is perfect, but, once again, you need to always remember:

Jesus doesn't expect us to be perfect; He just wants us to do our very best.

~Time to Pray~

God, it seems kind of hard to have **self-control** and be patient when someone isn't kind to me. I need your help and guidance. Please be with me as I try my best to overlook insults and respond with humility and grace. Thank you for always helping me!

Amen.

SELF-CONTROL SCENARIOS

What should you do if your friend tells you that his drawing is better than yours?

Should you tell him that his isn't good and yours is better?

HINT: The best thing to do is just smile and say, "Your picture is really good. **I think they're both good.**" That would display great **self-control** and please the Lord.

A Fruit of the Spirit

Transform Your Mind

"**2** Do not conform to the pattern of this world, but be transformed by the renewing of your mind. Then you will be able to test and approve what God's will is—his good, pleasing and perfect will."
Romans 12:2

Why do you think God doesn't want us to conform to this world?

What does "conform" even mean?

To conform means 'to be or become similar in form, nature, or character.'

God says that he doesn't want us to become like the things that don't respect his teachings. He doesn't want us to act like the people who don't love Him do. He doesn't want us to say words that don't glorify and honor Him.

Do you know who rules the world?

He is called the 'Prince of the World,' and He is the devil. Many things in this world tempt us and try to take our attention away from Jesus. That is the devil's goal. He doesn't want us to act like Jesus because He knows that if we do, we will be able to tell others about Him and expand the kingdom of Heaven!

Do you need to be worried and afraid of the devil?
Absolutely not.

God is the KING of Heaven *and* earth, and if we renew our minds and commit our lives to follow Him, He will always be there to protect us and shelter us from the temptations of the devil.

God will help us have self-control when we are tempted by things that distract us from Him.

The next time you are tempted to watch a movie that isn't good or say a word that you know you shouldn't say, remember to stop and ask God to give you self-control so that you can say 'no'!

A Fruit of the Spirit

~Time to Pray~

Lord, I am so glad that You are the King of Heaven and earth and that you are in control of everything. There is no one like You. When I am tempted to act in a way that isn't pleasing to You, please remind me that you've given me the gift of self-control and that I am strong enough to use it!

Amen.

SELF-CONTROL SCENARIOS

What would you do if your parents left you with a babysitter and your big sister or brother started trying to convince the babysitter that you were allowed to ride your scooter in the house, but you knew that it wasn't allowed?

Run the Race

"**24** Do you not know that in a race all the runners run, but only one gets the prize? Run in such a way as to get the prize. **25** Everyone who competes in the games goes into strict training. They do it to get a crown that will not last, but we do it to get a crown that will last forever."

1 Corinthians 9:24-25

Do you like to race your friends? Do you run super fast?

It's a lot of fun to have races, isn't it?

Have you ever gotten tired, or maybe your legs started hurting, and you decided to quit the race?

A Fruit of the Spirit

To win a race, an athlete has to train hard and take very good care of themselves while they prepare. They use *self-control* when it comes to how they eat and how much they train and exercise.

A good athlete never quits and keeps his or her eyes focused on the finish line.

The Bible says that we should live our lives as if we were running a race.

Do you know what are some things that you can do as a Christian to keep yourself focused on Jesus? Well, we need to pray every day, read our Bible, and make sure we are living in a way that honors and glorifies God.

Our ultimate goal should be to grow closer and closer to Jesus and to be excited about spending eternity with Him in Heaven someday. We need to keep our eyes on the prize *(Heaven),* work really hard, and *never give up.*

~Time to Pray~

Jesus, I am so grateful that someday, I will get to spend eternity in Heaven with You. Please help me keep my focus on You and never stop working hard to win the race. Thank you for being right beside me all the time, rooting for me to win, and helping me up when I fall. I love You, Lord.

Amen.

SELF-CONTROL SCENARIOS

Would it be better to wake up and ask Jesus to help you live like Him in the morning? Or would it be better to jump up and play video games right away?

If something happened that made you sad today, would it be better to cry and worry all day? Or would it be better to pray and ask Jesus to take care of you and give you peace?

As you go through your day, look for ways you can serve the Lord and include Him in your life.

A Fruit of the Spirit

15
His Grace is Sufficient

"⁹ But he said to me, 'My grace is sufficient for you, for my power is made perfect in weakness.' Therefore I will boast all the more gladly about my weaknesses, so that Christ's power may rest on me."
2 Corinthians 12:9

When we are weak, God is made strong.

That is a powerful statement. If we had everything all together, our lives were always perfect, and we never made mistakes, we wouldn't feel like we needed Jesus, would we? **We do need Him**, though, because we aren't perfect and mess up and make mistakes.

God gives us His grace.

That means that even when we lose our **self-control** and do something we know that we absolutely shouldn't do, God forgives us when we come to him to apologize, and it doesn't change how much He loves us at all!

Wow!

You don't need to walk around pretending you are perfect and don't have any weaknesses. God says that **His power is made perfect in our weaknesses,** so when you openly admit you have made a mistake, others can watch God change you and show off how mighty and powerful He is!

God's grace doesn't give us an excuse to purposely do the wrong thing all the time, though, does it? ***No, it doesn't.***

He wants us to always be working toward growing in Him and trying to follow his commands.

Use your God-given self-control to make good decisions, and when you fall, God will be right there to pick you up and help you try again.

~Time to Pray~

God, I am so thankful that You cover me with Your grace and love me still, even when I am weak and make mistakes. Please help me have **self-control** and always think about how I can honor you and obey you. Please show me the areas in my life where I need improvement and help me succeed in changing them! I love you, Lord.

Amen.

SELF-CONTROL SCENARIOS

If you make a mistake and do something you aren't supposed to do, should you try and pretend it didn't happen? Or should you **confess and pray for forgiveness?**

Is there anything that you've done recently that you feel you need to **ask forgiveness** for?

Remaining Calm

"**11** Fools give full vent to their rage,
but the wise bring calm in the end."
Proverbs 29:11

*Have you ever gotten frustrated because your
drawing didn't turn out the way you wanted?*

Or maybe you were right in the middle of
playing a game, and your mom asked you to clean
your room! Has that ever happened to you?

*Have you ever lost control and done something that
wasn't very nice because you were angry?*

We all lose self-control sometimes!

A Fruit of the Spirit

We lose our tempers and say and do things that we shouldn't because we are angry and frustrated. **Did you know that you can actually control those feelings?** You can't give in to every single emotional urge that you feel—especially the angry ones.

Angry people hurt people.

The Bible tells us not to give full vent to our rage. That means we shouldn't give it control of our actions! Don't let it rule your life! Jesus says that a wise person remains calm when they really want to yell and scream.

The next time you start to get frustrated and want to lash out at somebody, try a couple of these tips to help you remain calm

- **Pray** and ask Jesus to help you calm down.
- Go outside and **spend a minute in the fresh air**.
- **Take** some **deep breaths**.
- **Count to ten (10)** slowly.
- **Think** about something that makes you **happy**.
- If you have a pet, spend time **cuddling** him/her.

- **Hug someone** and release some of that frustration.

As you practice these helpful methods more and more, you'll start to learn how to have **self-control** and be slow to anger in challenging situations.

~Time to Pray~

Jesus, sometimes it's tough to remain calm when something makes me really angry. I need your help to have more **self-control** when I'm feeling frustrated. Please be with me and teach me how to be more like You.

Amen!

SELF-CONTROL SCENARIOS

Today we learned about lots of different things we can do when we are feeling angry. Can you name **three (3)** things that you could do if your friend broke one of your favorite toys?

Flee From Evil

"²⁷ Do not turn to the right or the left;
keep your foot from evil."
Proverbs 4:27

---

*What does it mean to **"keep your foot from evil?"***

That's kind of a funny thing to say, isn't it? Basically, it's another way of saying, "Stay away from things that are evil and not pleasing to the Lord."

What are some things that might be Considered evil *that you might be tempted by?*

Here are a few examples:

- Watching certain tv shows that **you know your parents disapprove of.**
- **Lying** to avoid getting in trouble for a mistake you made.
- **Stealing** something that doesn't belong to you.
- **Arguing with your parents** or teachers and **being disrespectful.**

Have you ever been tempted with any of these things?

I knew a little boy named Josh, and he was still learning how to have **self-control** and be honest. One day, he was playing with the curtains in his parents' room and accidentally broke them! And as he didn't want to get in trouble, he shoved the curtains under his parents' bed and didn't tell them.

Oh no!

When his mom found the curtains under the bed, do you think she was sadder about the fact that he broke the curtains or that he tried to hide what he did from her?

She was disappointed that he didn't feel like he could tell her the truth.

Your parents want you to be honest and tell them when you make the wrong decision.

Can you do that?

I know you can.

Remember to ask the Holy Spirit to give you self-control and help you say 'no'!

~Time to Pray~

God, thank you for blessing me with being able to come to You when I need help. Sometimes, it is really hard to say no to things I'm tempted by. Please help me to stay away from things that are evil and not pleasing to You.

Amen.

SELF-CONTROL SCENARIOS

What would you have done if you'd been in the room with Josh and seen him break the blinds and then hide them?

Watch and Pray

"**41** 'Watch and pray so that you will not fall into temptation. The spirit is willing, but the flesh is weak.'"
Matthew 26:41

Have you ever heard about Adam and Eve in the Bible? They were the first people that God created. And in the book of Genesis, it is explained how the devil tempted Eve with the forbidden fruit.

God told them that they could eat anything in the Garden of Eden *except* from the Tree of Good and Evil.

Imagine how they must have felt, looking at that tree with beautiful fruit on it, knowing they

A Fruit of the Spirit

couldn't eat it. That must have been very tempting. The devil knew that they were tempted, and he told them lies and convinced Eve to eat the fruit!

Eve didn't use self-control*. Her flesh was weak.*

God says that we need to always be watching and praying. We need to make sure that we are strong and ready to resist the devil's temptations. God is ready and willing to help us with that because He wants us to be happy and thriving, living our lives in a way that is pleasing to Him.

Your spirit is willing!

~Time to Pray~

God, I know that I will be tempted a lot in my life to do things that aren't pleasing to You. I pray that you would continue to help me grow stronger and stronger in my faith. Please help me to exercise self-control every single day as I learn to be more like You. Thank you for being my strength when I am weak.

Amen.

SELF-CONTROL SCENARIOS

If I put a plate of donuts in front of you right now but told you that you couldn't eat them and then I left the room, what would you do?

Would you be tempted to eat the donuts? Or do you think that you would be able to resist them?

What is something that you could do to help you have self-control?

19

Stay Strong

"**12** For our struggle is not against flesh and
blood, but against the rulers, against the
authorities, against the powers of this dark world
and against the spiritual forces of evil in the
heavenly realms."
Ephesians 6:12

Lincoln loves to play games on his electronic tablet. It's one of his favorite things to do, but his mom has a very strict rule regarding its use: he isn't ever allowed to bring it into his bedroom because she wants to be able to see what he is doing on it.

One night at bedtime, his mom was busy and asked him to put himself to bed, and all of a sudden, he had an idea.

"Mom would never notice if I brought my tablet to bed with me tonight," he thought.

The devil was tempting Lincoln.

Oh no!

Unfortunately, instead of practicing his self-control, he stuffed the tablet under his shirt, gave his mom a goodnight kiss, and snuck it into his room. He played on his tablet for hours that night, and when his mom peeked in to check on him, he quickly hid it under his blankets.

Have you ever disobeyed your parents?

If so, did you feel bad afterward?

When Lincoln woke up in the morning, he felt tired, guilty, and sad. He knew what he had done was wrong. The Holy Spirit was convicting him, and he knew he had to confess to his mom.

She was disappointed by his actions, and he got punished, but she prayed with him and asked Jesus to give him self-control so that he could resist the devil's temptations.

A Fruit of the Spirit

~Time to Pray~

Jesus, I understand that I need to be on guard and ready to resist the lies and temptations of the devil. When I am tempted to disobey my parents and do something that I know I'm not supposed to do, please help me say 'no'! I want to be like You, Lord. Make me strong.

Amen.

SELF-CONTROL SCENARIOS

What would you have done if you had been with Lincoln when he had done that?

Would you have let him do it?
Would you have tried to convince him not to do it? Would you have gone and told his mom?

Maybe, you would have just told your mom when you went home so she could call his mom?

Often, there is more than one way to do the right thing. We just need to stop and pray that the Lord will show us how to be honest and love others at the same time.

God Is On Our Side

> "⁴ You, dear children, are from God and have overcome them, because the one who is in you is greater than the one who is in the world."
> **1 John 4:4**

We have talked a lot about resisting temptations from the devil. It is crucial to be strong and steadfast in the Lord. However, it is equally as important to understand that God is on our side.

God is your protector against all evil.

God is much more powerful than the devil, and we are so lucky to have him on our team because

A Fruit of the Spirit

we are never alone in our struggles! We don't have to fight all alone. We have the most mighty king to protect us and carry us when we are weak.

If God is for us, who can be against us?

The answer is no one.

There isn't a single person or thing that can overcome our God. We may have struggles and temptations, but in the end, if we are followers of Christ, we will have victory!

GOD IS YOUR REAL-LIFE SUPERHERO!

When we face temptation, we need to pray and ask God to help us be strong. He will always remind us of a verse in the Bible—His Words—that will help us be strong and say "no."

The next time you're having a hard time doing the right thing, remember that you're on **God's** team, and it's so important to obey His words!

You can be strong and courageous because you have Jesus on your side.

~Time to Pray~

God, thank you for choosing me to be on your team! I am so grateful that I have you on my side. When I'm feeling discouraged, please help me be strong and remember that I'm not alone. In Jesus' name, Amen!

SELF-CONTROL SCENARIOS

It is so important to have God's words memorized so that in times of trouble, we can find shelter in them over and over.

Can you say today's bible verse? Try saying it a few times and see if you can memorize it!

21
Walk in the Spirit

"¹⁷ For the flesh desires what is contrary to the Spirit, and the Spirit what is contrary to the flesh. They are in conflict with each other, so that you are not to do whatever you want."

Galatians 5:17

As Christians, we are supposed to live our lives in a way that glorifies God. That means that there are going to be times in your life when you'll have to say 'no' to your fleshly desires, even when you really don't want to.

I know a little girl named Lily, who really struggled with that for a while. She was always getting in trouble with her parents because she was doing things she wasn't supposed to!

One day, she was sitting at the table doing her homework, but she didn't feel like it at all! She just wanted to be playing with her toys instead of being sat, bored with school things. So, not having **self-control,** every single time her mom looked away, she left the table to play with her toys!

Her mom was so frustrated!

In the end, her mom had enough of Lily's misbehavior and grounded her from playing with those toys. And you know what's worse? That it ended up taking her all night to finish her homework, and she didn't get to play before bed at all!

Have you ever had a hard time focusing on your schoolwork because you just want to play instead?

You're going to see that you'll be able to use your **self-control** in lots of different scenarios throughout your life. You'll use it when you're choosing what to eat, how you speak to your siblings, what television shows you watch, the music you listen to, and even how you act when it's time to do school work!

Remember that it's important to pray and read your Bible. Doing this feeds your spirit instead of your flesh and helps you to be able to be strong when you're feeling weak!

~Time to Pray~

Lord, I pray today that you would help me to have self-control. I understand that, in my life, I will always battle between listening to my flesh and listening to my spirit. Please help me to always listen to the Holy Spirit!

Amen.

SELF-CONTROL SCENARIOS

What would you do if you had just gotten in trouble with your parents and you looked over, and your brother or sister was smiling at you?

What would be the **wrong** thing to do? What would be the right thing to do?

Control Your Thoughts

"⁸ Finally, brothers and sisters, whatever is true, whatever is noble, whatever is right, whatever is pure, whatever is lovely, whatever is admirable—if anything is excellent or praiseworthy—think about such things. ⁹ Whatever you have learned or received or heard from me, or seen in me—put it into practice. And the God of peace will be with you."
Philippians 4:8-9

Carter was finally ready to try riding his bike without training wheels. He really liked to be good at things, so he was really afraid that he wouldn't be able to do it.

A Fruit of the Spirit

He swung his leg over and tried to take off, but instantly, he fell. Instead of getting up and trying again, he ran into the house, threw himself on his bed, and started thinking some untrue thoughts.

"I'm so dumb," he thought, while a tear fell from his eye. "Everyone else can ride their bikes, so why can't I? I'm not good at anything!"

Jesus says that we are supposed to think true thoughts. Those thoughts that Carter was thinking about himself were not true at all!

Big thoughts can be scary and overwhelming!

It's important to remember that just because a thought enters your mind doesn't mean it's true!

The next time untrue thoughts enter your head, you need to remember to stop and pray! Ask the Holy Spirit to help you think thoughts that are true and right. Never be afraid to tell your parents or teacher that you're having trouble thinking good things about yourself.

You are not alone!

~Time to Pray~

Jesus, sometimes the devil puts thoughts in my head that aren't true about myself, and it makes me feel bad. Thank you for showing me that they aren't true! Please help me think about things that are true about myself. I'm so glad that I have you, Lord!

Amen.

SELF-CONTROL SCENARIOS

Sometimes we do things by accident. If you fell and spilled your cereal all over the ground, it would be easy to get frustrated with yourself, wouldn't it?

What could you say to yourself that would help you feel better?

A Fruit of the Spirit

23

Roaring Lions

"⁸ Be alert and of sober mind. Your enemy the devil prowls around like a roaring lion looking for someone to devour."
1 Peter 5:8

Have you ever been to a zoo before?

If so, did you get to see the lions?

Have you ever seen a lion trying to hunt for its lunch?

When a lion is hunting, it watches its prey for a while, and then, when its prey is vulnerable and unexpecting, the lion pounces!

The same can be said about the devil. He waits until we are weak, and then he tries to get us to turn away from Jesus. It's so important for us to be strong and focused on the truth—Jesus.

"Do not fear, for I am with you; do not be dismayed, for I am your God. I will strengthen you and help you; I will uphold you with my righteous right hand."
Isaiah 41:10

You don't have to be afraid of the devil. You serve a mighty God who is way more powerful. Keep your eyes focused on Him, and he will help you resist the devil's lies and temptations!

~Time to Pray~

Thank you, Lord, for not giving me a spirit of fear. Thank you because I can lean on you when I'm afraid and when the devil is tempting me. I pray that You will hold me close and that I will be strong and resist the devil. I will keep my eyes on You, Jesus.

Amen.

A Fruit of the Spirit

SELF-CONTROL SCENARIOS

Thunder and lighting can be scary sometimes, can't it? When you're lying in your bed at night, and a thunderstorm starts, what is something you could do to practice self-control and not let fear take over?

24
God Makes You Strong

"¹³ I can do all this through him who gives me strength."
Philippians 4:13

Are you strong? Really, really, strong?

Let me see those muscles.

Pretty impressive!

What does being strong mean to you? Did you know that besides being strong physically and having big muscles, you can also be strong spiritually?

You can be strong in your mind!

A little girl named Isla was having trouble controlling her thoughts at bedtime. The second her parents turned out the light, she started feeling afraid. She was sure something was hiding in her closet or under her bed. Something scary.

But, no matter how scared she was, Isla knew the truth. She knew that Jesus protected her always and that she was safe in her room, and the devil didn't like that! He was trying to get her to forget that she had Jesus in her heart and to have a spirit of fear.

After a few nights, Isla realized that she could ask Jesus to take away her fear! So she closed her eyes and whispered a bible verse she had learned in Sunday school: "When I am afraid, I will trust in You, Jesus."

When we are weak, He is strong!

Jesus can make you strong in your mind. All you have to do is pray and ask him to help you. When you can't stop thinking about something you aren't supposed to, or when you have the same scary thoughts or worries every day, call out to Jesus. He loves you and wants to help you.

Aren't we lucky to have Him?

~Time to Pray~

Dear Lord, today, I want to ask you to help me control my thoughts. I pray that you'd help me think only things that are true and honoring to You. When I feel afraid, when I am tempted to think untrue thoughts about myself, or spend too much time thinking about something that distracts me from You, I pray that you'd help me change my focus to You. Thank you, Jesus.

Amen!

SELF-CONTROL SCENARIOS

What is something you would have done to help Isla if you'd been there when she was scared?

A Fruit of the Spirit

25

Taking Offense

"**11** A person's wisdom yields patience;
it is to one's glory to overlook an offense."
Proverbs 19:11

Do you think Jesus ever gets offended?

In order to answer that question, let's look at the definition of that word. What does being offended mean?

Being offended is to be resentful or annoyed, typically as a result of a perceived insult.

Does that sound like something Jesus does? **No, it doesn't.**

In the Bible, there were many times where He could have been resentful or angry, but he chose to show them grace and forgiveness time and time again.

Even to those who hung him on the cross.

We are called to be like Jesus. That means that we need to learn to have **self-control** when it comes to being offended by others. Has anyone done anything to you that may have caused you to feel offended?

It is essential to understand the difference between someone intentionally doing something mean to you, and understanding when they are just teasing or saying something without thinking first. We can't read each other's thoughts, so sometimes it's hard to figure out someone's motive!

When we learn how to NOT take offense to everything, our lives will become much more peaceful and happy.

~Time to Pray~

Jesus, I confess that I have taken offense to things too quickly, and it's taken away some of my joy. I pray that you would show me who I am in You so that I wouldn't care as much what other people think. I'm blessed that I can come to You for help and trust that you'll change my heart.

Amen!

SELF-CONTROL SCENARIOS

What if you told a friend that you didn't like a certain song, and then they started singing it! Do you think that is being mean, or do you think that is just teasing?

HINT: They're only teasing. You just need to laugh and be thankful that you have a friend to joke around with.

26
Taking Our Thoughts Captive

"⁵ We demolish arguments and every pretension
that sets itself up against the knowledge of God, and
we take captive every thought to make it
obedient to Christ."
2 Corinthians 10:5

Do you remember Adam and Eve from the Bible? Well, there, it is also explained how they had two sons. Their names were Cain and Abel. Cain was very jealous of his brother because he always seemed to be doing everything right.

One day, God decided to help Cain and told him to take his thoughts captive and focus on good thoughts instead of bad thoughts (jealousy and

A Fruit of the Spirit

anger), but Cain did not listen, and his thoughts caused him to do some horrible things.

Do you have trouble with your thoughts? Do you focus on too many negative things?

If so, you need to pray that Jesus will renew your mind (Romans 12:2).

Jesus is so powerful and loves you so much.

If you ask Him to help you have positive thoughts and focus on the truth, He will help you! Sometimes, we just can't do it alone!

The Bible says we are to focus on things that are "true, noble, right, pure, lovely, and admirable."

Can you think of some things that are lovely?

How about things that are admirable?

The next time you start to have a negative thought, stop yourself and think about those things instead! If you practice doing this every day, it will become a habit, and you will feel so much happier.

This will take a lot of self-control, but you can do it!

~Time to Pray~

God, today I learned that I am supposed to actually *think* about my *thoughts*! I have never considered that before, but now I realize how important it is. I can't do what you have called me to do if I'm always walking around thinking sad or angry thoughts. Please, come and change my thoughts and renew my mind. Thank you, Jesus.

Amen.

SELF-CONTROL SCENARIOS

Just like Cain and Able, there may come a time where your brother or sister gets something that you really wanted.

What is something really nice that you could say to them even though you're feeling jealous?

A Fruit of the Spirit

27

GOD IS FOR US

"**31** What, then, shall we say in response to these things? If God is for us, who can be against us?"
Romans 8:31

Do you think there is anyone or anything that could separate us from the love of God?

Absolutely not! No way!

Even the biggest, strongest person in the world is not more powerful than Jesus Christ. Not even a terrible sin or secret could turn God away from you.

Have you ever made a mistake?

Everyone has! We were born sinners, saved by God's grace.

When you make a mistake, do you feel ashamed? Embarrassed? Have you ever wanted to hide it from God?

God doesn't ever want you to turn away from Him! He wants you to be brave and come to Him and ask forgiveness when you sin!

This is another opportunity for you to use self-control. It's natural for us to want to hide when we sin, but the next time you catch yourself doing something wrong, you need to STOP AND PRAY!

If you can succeed in stopping yourself when you're about to do something wrong, you will be using self-control, and God will bless you for that.

You won't regret it.

A Fruit of the Spirit

~Time to Pray~

Jesus, thank you for the gift of self-control. Today, I have been challenged to pay attention when I'm about to do something wrong and stop and pray instead. I feel like this is going to be kind of hard. I pray that you would give me the strength and determination. Thank you for always being there to help me.

Amen.

SELF-CONTROL SCENARIOS

What would you do if you were at a store and you looked down and saw a candy bar on the floor? Would you pick it up knowing it would fit in your pocket and your parent wasn't looking?

Would you steal it? Or would you be able to be strong and say no?

28

The Truth Will Set You Free

"³¹To the Jews who had believed him, Jesus said, "If you hold to my teaching, you are really my disciples. ³²Then you will know the truth, and the truth will set you free."
John 8:31-32

Do you know what a habit is?

It is something that you do over and over again, and it becomes hard to stop. You can have good habits, and you can have bad habits.

Bad habits often distract us from doing what God has called us to do.

There was a little boy named Kevin, and he had a terrible habit. Do you want to know what it was? He really wanted other kids to like him, so he started making up lies so that they would think he was cool.

At first, it was little things, like how he had gotten a new game, when he really hadn't or that he went to a fun place that he actually hadn't been to.

Eventually, though, the lies grew and grew until he was telling huge lies! The lies were so big that everyone knew that they weren't true, and he got a reputation for being a liar.

He never meant for it to get so out of hand, but that is what happens when we start bad habits!

What are some other things that could be considered bad habits?

Let me give you some examples:

- Playing video games for *hours and hours* without stopping.
- *Eating more than you need to* and making yourself feel sick.
- *Being lazy* about doing your schoolwork.

- **Fighting** with your siblings.
- **Biting** your fingernails.

Do you think you have any bad habits?

You know what? **God *can* and *wants* to set you free from them!** He wants you to have an abundantly joyful life that pleases him and makes you happy! It's no fun feeling guilty. Let's pray and ask him to set us free from our bad habits and help us learn good habits instead!

~Time to Pray~

Jesus, I pray that you will show me what I have been doing over and over again that isn't pleasing to You. I pray that you would give me the strength and the **self-control** to turn my bad habits into good habits. Thank you for setting me free! In Your name, we pray, **Amen**.

A Fruit of the Spirit

SELF-CONTROL SCENARIOS

What should you do if you're doing your schoolwork and you notice that the answers are in the back of the book?

Would looking at them and writing them down be considered cheating?

What if no one was around to see you do it?
Should you?

29
Put On Your Armor

"[10]Finally, be strong in the Lord and in his mighty power. [11]Put on the full armor of God, so that you can take your stand against the devil's schemes."
Ephesians 6:10-11

Have you ever held a sword in your hand?

Do you know what it's like to put on a full suit of armor?

In the Bible, a man named Paul, one of the **twelve (12)** Apostles of Jesus, talks about how we are supposed to put on the full armor of God!

But, how do we do that?

A Fruit of the Spirit

Do you have armor lying around somewhere in your bedroom?

I sure don't!

In this scripture, Paul is talking about real armor, but he uses it as a metaphor to teach us how to prepare for spiritual warfare and how to fight against the devil.

When you ride your bike, skateboard, or roller skates, do you wear protective gear? Jesus wants us to have protective gear for our life! That is why he gives us the full armor of God.

lets put on our armor and TAKE A STAND FOR JESUS!

~Time to Pray~

Jesus, I pray that you would give me discernment. Help me to always be aware of the devil's lies and to know the truth. Thank you for giving me special armor so that I can fight against evil. Help me be strong in You, Lord!

Amen.

SELF-CONTROL SCENARIOS

Do you think you are strong enough to win against sin and stand up to the devil?

What should you do if you believe that the devil is telling you lies and you are worried that it might be true?

Stand Firm

"**14**Stand firm then, with the belt of truth buckled around your waist, with the breastplate of righteousness in place,"
Ephesians 6:14

Have you ever heard of the Belt of Truth?

This is the first piece of armor that we are going to learn about. The Belt of Truth is where we store all of our knowledge of God. It protects us from the devil's lies. If he tries to tell us something untrue or tries to tempt us, we can reach into our Belt of Truth and pull out something TRUE, like a verse from the Bible, and use it to fight against him.

What a great tool to have!

Can you pretend you're putting on a great big Belt of Truth?

*Do you want to **win against sin?***

Jesus says that when we do what he wants us to do instead of sinning, we are putting on the Breastplate of Righteousness!

How do you know what Jesus wants you to do?

The Holy Spirit tells you.

All you have to do is stop and pray. Listen for a quiet whisper in your heart.

A little boy named Greyson was so excited because his mom said he could go to his neighbors' house for 1 hour. She told him to watch the time and be home exactly when he was supposed to.

When the time came, he told his friend that it was time to go, and his friend begged and pleaded for him to stay! He even offered to give him one of his favorite toys if he chose to stay!

A Fruit of the Spirit

What do you think Greyson chose to do?

He stopped for a second and thought about it. He really wanted that toy because he didn't have anything like it at home, but suddenly, he felt very sure of what he needed to do. God wanted him to respect his mom, and he knew that obeying God was the best thing to do. He said goodbye to his friend and went home.

We are all put in sticky situations like that in our lives. The important thing to do is walk toward obedience to God and put on that special breastplate of righteousness.

What a great reward!

~Time to Pray~

Lord, I pray that if I'm ever put into a situation like that where I am really tempted to disobey, You would help me hear the Holy Spirit telling me what to do. I pray that I could proudly wear the breastplate of righteousness and honor you, Jesus.

Amen.

SELF-CONTROL SCENARIOS

Have you ever been put in a scenario like Greyson was in?

Would you have taken the toy he promised and stayed longer? Or would you have obeyed and gone home?

What is something that Greyson could have said to his neighbor before leaving that would have taught him about Jesus and obedience?

31
Get Your Feet Ready

"¹⁵ and with your feet fitted with the readiness that
comes from the gospel of peace"
Ephesians 6:15

Do you have a favorite pair of shoes?

What do they look like?

*I'll bet you wear sandals when it's warm outside,
don't you?*

In the Bible, the Romans wore sandals all of the time. Even in battle! Their sandals had spikes on the bottom that dug into the ground so that they could stand firm and keep from falling.

The Apostle Paul tells us to have our 'feet fitted with the Gospel of Peace.' It's called the Gospel of Peace because Jesus made peace with us when He died on the cross.

Imagine putting on those sandals that the Romans wore with spikes on the bottom. God wants you to be ready, with your feet firmly planted on the ground, to tell people about Jesus and preach the Gospel confidently. Yes, even as a child, you can share God's word and make a difference in His Kingdom!

Adorn your feet with the Gospel of Peace, study God's word, and tell people all about Him!

Sometimes, it isn't easy to open up our Bibles and spend time learning about the Gospel and about who God is. Some days it may take a lot of self-control to pick up our Bibles instead of our video games or favorite toys.

You are equipped and READY to use your God-given self-control.

A Fruit of the Spirit

~Time to Pray~

Lord, thank you for teaching me **self-control**. I know that I won't always be perfect, but I will always try my best. Help me be brave and strong as I stand up for my faith in You and tell others about Your Gospel. I am your soldier!

Amen.

SELF-CONTROL SCENARIOS

What would you say if someone told you that God isn't real?
That's a big question, isn't it?

Would you clothe your feet with the Gospel of Peace and tell them proudly that he is real and that you love him very much?

Perfectly Protected

"¹⁶ In addition to all this, take up the shield of faith, with which you can extinguish all the flaming arrows of the evil one. ¹⁷Take the helmet of salvation and the sword of the Spirit, which is the word of God."
Ephesians 6:16-17

A special verse in the Bible says this:

"Do not be afraid of the king of Babylon, whom you now fear. Do not be afraid of him, declares the Lord, for I am with you and will save you and deliver you from his hands."

A Fruit of the Spirit

Jesus clarifies that he doesn't want us to be afraid of anything and that he will always protect us. He gave us His special armor that we need to remember to put on every day!

The last three pieces of armor we will learn about are The Shield of Faith, The Helmet of Salvation, and The Sword of the Spirit.

Let's take a closer look at these.

The Shield of Faith that the Apostle Paul is talking about is presumed to be like the shields that the Romans used in war. They were SO big that they covered their whole bodies! The Shield of Faith is so big and powerful that it protects us from the devil's "flaming arrows" of lies and doubt. It helps us to keep our faith in Jesus even if the devil tries to make us doubt Him.

The Helmet of Salvation protects our head and our thoughts. Jesus died on the cross for us so that we could be saved and live with him forever! The devil will try to convince us that Jesus doesn't love us and that we aren't going to Heaven. If we have asked Jesus into our hearts, ***then this is not true!*** We have to wear our protective gear and stand firm!

Lastly, Jesus gave us **The Sword of the Spirit,** which is the Bible. It's so important to read it and learn about God. We need to know it well to always be ready to protect ourselves against the devil's lies.

Learning how to use the full armor of God might be challenging!

It might take a while to get into the habit of doing what Jesus wants us to do rather than what *we* want to do, to pick up our bibles every day and memorize His words, and to ignore the devil's lies.

However, you are a son or daughter of Christ, and you have learned a lot about self-control. You can do hard things because you have the help of our Lord and Savior.

He is proud of You

He loves You

He will help you.

You've got this!

A Fruit of the Spirit

~Time to Pray~

Jesus, thank you for teaching me and being patient with me as I learn how to use **Self-Control**. Help me have my feet firmly planted and my mind focused on only You. Use me, Lord, that I might help further Your Kingdom. In Jesus' name, I pray, *Amen.*

SELF-CONTROL SCENARIO

Do you understand what **The Armor of God** is?

Are you confident in your ability to use **Self-Control?**

If you make a mistake and lose your **Self-Control,** will **God forgive you?**

HINT: Yes! He will. He will always forgive you because He loves you so much. Just get back up and try again!

Coming Soon

Anchored in Peace

A Fruit of the Spirit Devotional for Kids

JENNA MAYE THOMPSON

Made in the USA
Monee, IL
02 August 2022

10774567R00064